Mel Bay presents Fun w

Ukulele

Fun with the Ukulele Level 2 *by Bill Bay*

FUN WITH STRUMS—UKULELE, is a book designed to aid the beginning Uke player in playing strums applicable to folk and bluegrass music. A variety of keys are studied and the student will gain versatility in playing chord progressions. The keys of G, E minor, C, A minor, D, E, A, F, and D minor are presented. This book is an ideal follow-up to Mel Bay's FUN WITH THE UKULELE. It is our hope that upon completion of this text the student will have gained considerable ability and enjoyment.

TABLE OF CONTENTS

1 2 3 4 5 6 7 8 9 0

*See page 2

SYMBOLS USED

STRUM SYMBOLS

A SWEEPING DOWN STROKE ACROSS THE STRINGS. THE MOTION IS FROM THE BIGGEST OR LOWER TO THE SMALLEST OR HIGHER STRINGS.

A DOWN STROKE IMMEDIATELY FOLLOWED BY AN UP STROKE OF EQUAL LENGTH.

TUNING

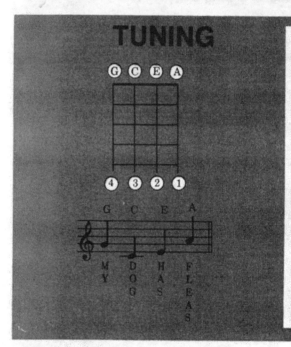

EXPLANATION OF CHORD SYMBOLS

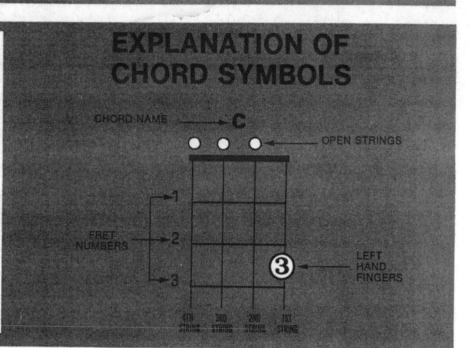

THE SIGNATURES

C OR **4/4** (4 BEATS PER MEASURE)
(A QUARTER NOTE RECEIVES ONE BEAT)
COUNT: 1-2-3-4, 1-2-3-4, ETC.

2/4 (2 BEATS PER MEASURE)
(A QUARTER NOTE RECEIVES ONE BEAT)
COUNT: 1-2, 1-2, 1-2, ETC.

3/4 (3 BEATS PER MEASURE)
(A QUARTER NOTE RECEIVES ONE BEAT)
COUNT: 1-2-3, 1-2-3, ETC.

6/8 (6 BEATS PER MEASURE)
(AN EIGHTH NOTE RECEIVES ONE BEAT)
COUNT: 1-2-3-4-5-6, 1-2-3-4-5-6 ETC.
(ACCENT BEATS 1 AND 4)

CHORDS IN G

THE 3 BASIC CHORDS IN THE KEY OF G ARE: G, C, and D7.

G

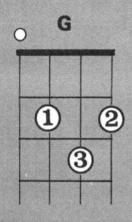

C

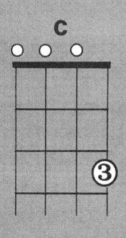

D7

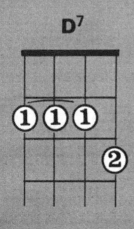

4

STRUM # 1

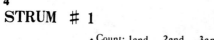

Using the thumb or pick, strum down across the strings on each beat.

Battle Hymn of the Republic

Verse

1. Mine eyes have seen the glo - ry of the com - ing of the Lord, He is

tram - pling out the vin - tage where the grapes of wrath are stored, He has

loosed the fate - ful light - ning of His ter - ri ble swift sword, His

truth is march - ing on. Glo - ry, glo - ry, Hal - le

lu - jah! Glo - ry, glo - ry, Hal - le - lu - jah!

Glo - ry, glo - ry, Hal - le lu - jah! His truth is march - ing on.

2. I have seen Him in the watch fires of a hundred circling camps.
They have builded Him an altar in the evening dews and damps.
I have read His righteous sentence by the dim of flaring lamps,
His truth is marching on.

3. In the beauty of the lilies, Christ was born across the sea,
With a glory in His bosom that transfigures you and me;
As He died to make men holy, Let us die to make men free,
While God is marching on.

STRUM # 2

With this strum, strum down on beat 1 and back up on the "and" count of beat 1. Strum down on the remaining beats.

Hush Little Baby

2. If that billy Goat won't pull,

mama's Gonna buy you a cart and bull.

If that cart and bull turn o'er.

mama's Gonna buy you a dog named rover.

3. If that dog named rover won't bark.

Mama's gonna buy you a horse and cart.

If that horse and cart break down,

You'll still be the sweetest little baby in town.

6

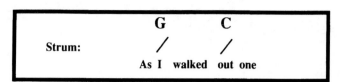

The Bold Fisherman

Sea Song

STRUM # 4

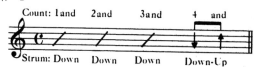

With this strum, strum down across the strings on the first 3 beats. On the 4th beat, strum down and up.

Bile 'Dem Cabbage Down

Chorus:
Bile dem cab-bage down, down, Turn dem hoe cakes round. The on-ly song that I could sing was bile dem cab-bage down.

Verse:
1. Went up on the moun-tain just to give my horn a blow, Thought I heard my true love say, "Yon-der comes my beau."

Verses

2. Took my gal to the black-smith shop
   To have her mouth made small,
   She turned around a time or two
   and swallowed show and all.

3. Possum in a 'simmon tree,
   Raccoon on the ground,
   Raccoon says, "You son-of-a-gun,
   Shake some 'simmons down!"

4. Someone stole my old 'coon dog
   Wish they'd bring him back
   He chased the big hogs thru the fence
   And the little ones thru the crack.

5. Met a possum in the road
   Blind as he could be,
   Jumped the fence and whipped my dog.
   And bristled up at me.

6. Once I had an old gray mule,
   His name was Siman Slick
   He'd roll his eyes and back his ears,
   And how that mule would kick!

7. I've heard some folks tell
   There's gold in them thar hills,
   But I lived up there forty years
   And all I seen was stills!

STRUM # 5

With this strum, strum down across the strings on the first beat. Strum down and back on the second. And strum down on the third and fourth beats.

Down By The Riverside

2. I'm gonna join hands with everyone, etc.

3. I'm gonna put on my long white robe, etc.

4. I'm gonna talk with the Prince of Peace, etc.

STRUM # 6

Strum down on beats 1 and 2. Strum down-up on beat 3.

Amazing Grace

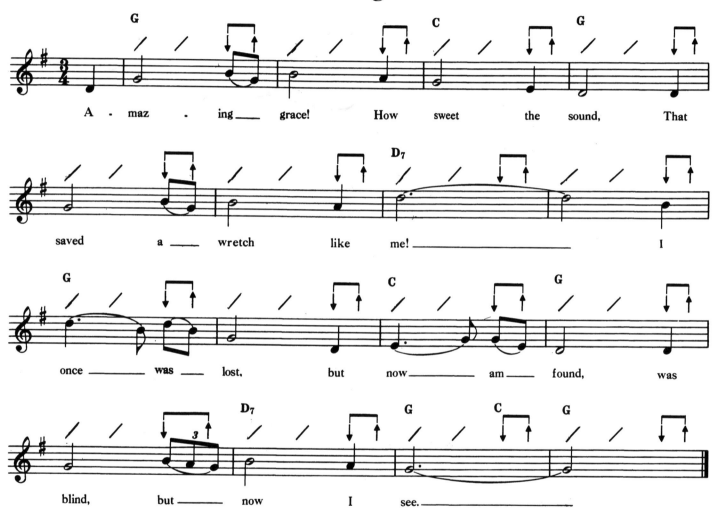

A - maz - ing ___ grace! How sweet the sound, That saved a ___ wretch like me! ___ I once ___ was ___ lost, but now ___ am ___ found, was blind, but ___ now I see. ___

2.   'Twas grace that taught my heart to fear
And grace my fears relieved;
How precious did that grace appear,
The hour I first believed!

3.   'Thru many dangers, Toils and snares,
I have already come;
'Tis grace hath brought me safe thus far,
And grace will lead me home.

4.   When we've been there ten thousand years,
Bright shining as the sun,
We've no less days to sing God's praise
Than when we first begun.

KEY OF E MINOR

THE THREE BASIC CHORDS IN THE KEY OF E MINOR ARE: Em, Am, and B7.

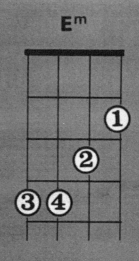

E^m

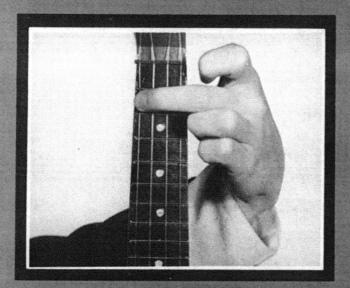

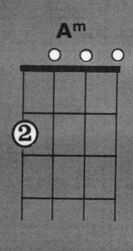

A^m

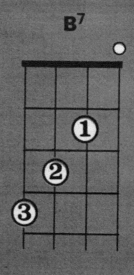

B^7

STRUM # 7

Strum down on beats 1 and 2. Strum down-up on beat 3 and strum down on the fourth beat.

Wade in the Water

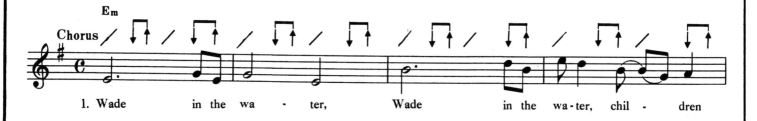

1. Wade in the wa - ter, Wade in the wa - ter, chil - dren

Wade in the wa - ter, God's gon - na trou - ble these wa - ters.

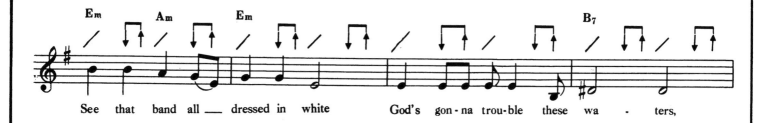

See that band all __ dressed in white God's gon - na trou - ble these wa - ters,

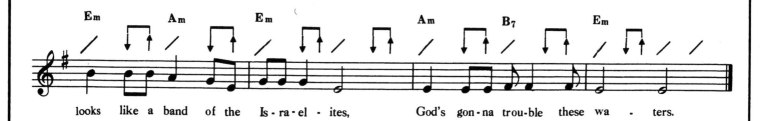

looks like a band of the Is - ra - el - ites, God's gon - na trou - ble these wa - ters.

Em Am Em
2. See that band all dressed in red,
B7
God's gonna trouble these waters,
Em Am Em
Looks like a band that Moses led,
Am B7 Em
God's gonna trouble these waters.

THE D CHORD

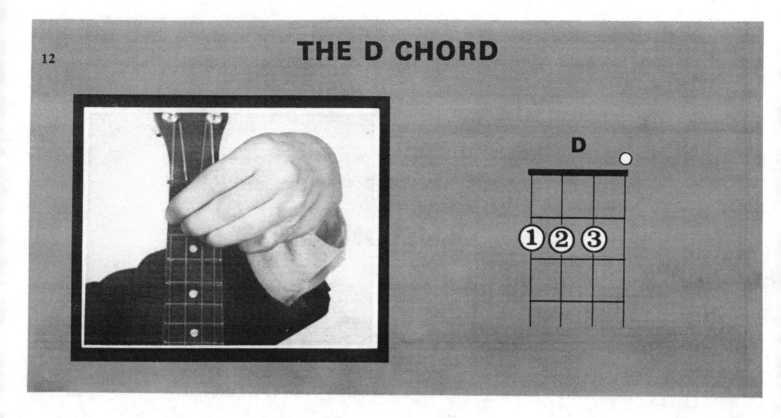

STRUM # 8 HARP STRUM

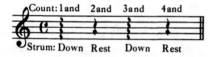

The harp strum is a slow, gradual strum down across the strings. It is very effective on ballads and slower songs. Each note of the chord should ring out clearly. The symbol for the harp strum is: Strum down on beats 1 and 3. Rest on beats 2 and 4. (Rest — don't strum but let chord continue to ring.)

Black is the Color of My True Love's Hair

1. Black, black. black is the col·or of my true love's hair._____ Her

face is like a paint·ing rare, The · blu · est eyes and the lo · ve · li · est hands._____

Black, black, black is the col·or of my true love's hair._____

STRUM # 9

This is a two measure strum pattern. In the 1st measure, strum down on beat 1 and down-up on beat 2. In the next measure, strum down-up on both beats.

Oh, Sinner Man

1. Oh, sin-ner man, where you gon-na run - to?

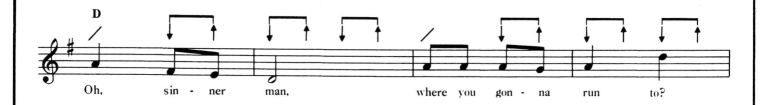

Oh, sin-ner man, where you gon-na run to?

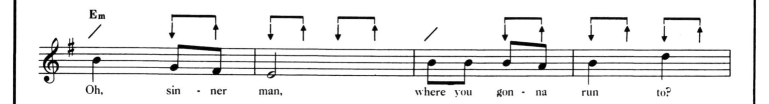

Oh, sin-ner man, where you gon-na run to?

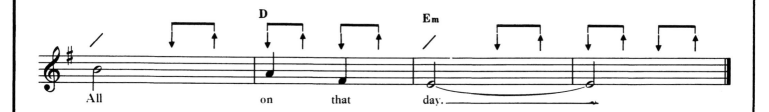

All on that day.

2. Run to the rock, the rock was a-melting,　(3 times)
All on that day.

3. Run to the sea, the sea was a-boiling,　(3 times)
All on that day.

4. Run to the moon, the moon was a-bleeding,　(3 times)
All on that day.

5. Run to the Lord, Lord won't you hide me?　(3 times)
All on that day.

6. Run to the Devil, Devil was a-waiting,　(3 times)
All on that day.

7. Oh sinner man, you oughta been a-praying,　(3 times)
All on that day.

THE B MINOR CHORD

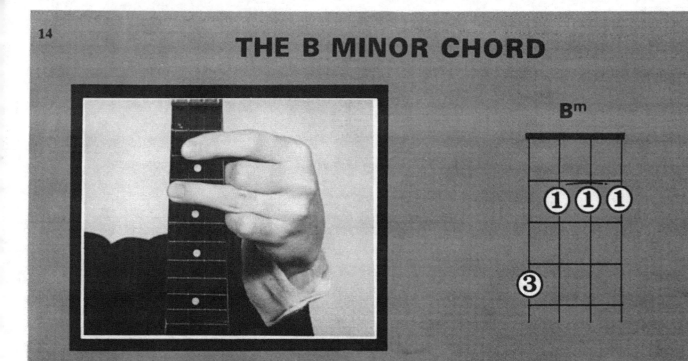

Bm

STRUM # 10

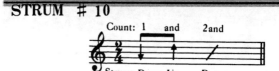

Count: 1 and 2and

Strum: Down-Up Down

This is another 2/4 time strum. Strum down-up on the 1st beat. And strum down on the second beat.

Shady Grove

Lively tempo
Chorus

1. Sha - dy Grove, my lit - tle love, Sha - da Grove, I say,

Sha - dy Grove, my lit - tle love, Bound for the Sha - dy Grove.

Verses:

Em   D
1. Apples in the summer time,
Em
Peaches in the fall,
Bm   D
If I can't get the girl I want,
Em   D   Em
I won't have none at all.

Em   D
2. Fatnin' hogs in the pen,
Em
Corn to feed them on,
Bm   D
All I want's a pretty little woman
Em   D   Em
To feed them while I'm gone.

Em   D
3. Shady grove, my pretty little love,
Em
Shady grove, my darlin!,
Bm   D
Shady grove, my pretty little love,
Em D Em
I'll go down to Harlan.

THE KEY OF C

THE THREE BASIC CHORDS IN THE KEY OF C ARE: C, F, and G7.

C

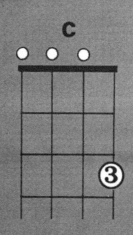

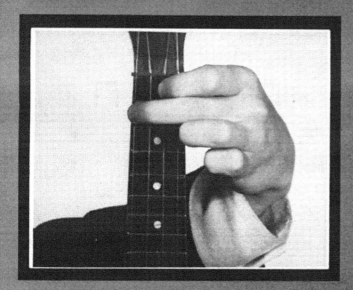

F

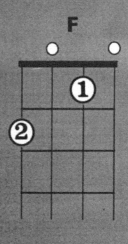

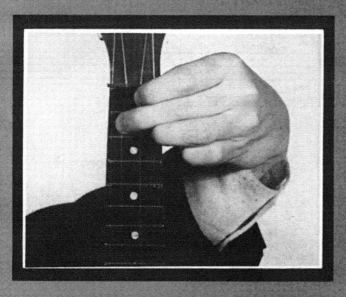

G⁷

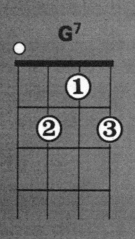

STRUM # 11

Strum down on beat 1. Strum down-up on beats 2 and 3. Strum down on beat 4.

Wildwood Flower

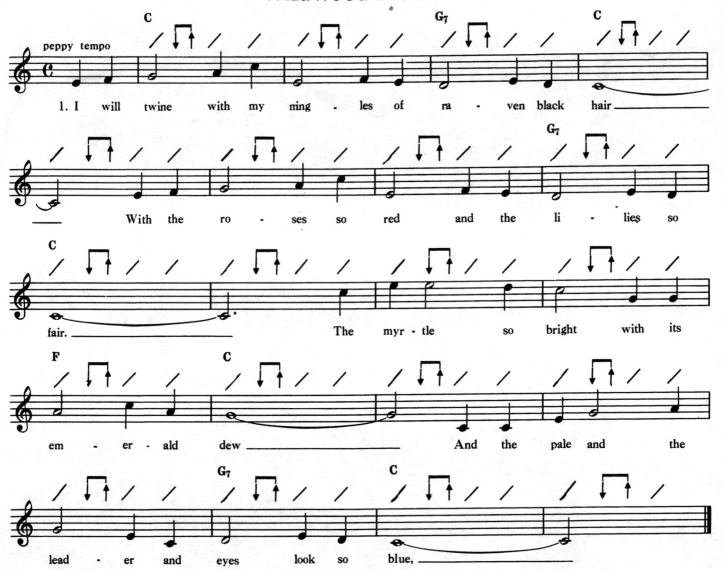

1. I will twine with my ming-les of ra-ven black hair ___ With the ro-ses so red and the li-lies so fair. ___ The myr-tle so bright with its em-er-ald dew ___ And the pale and the lead-er and eyes look so blue, ___

2. I will dance, I will sing and my life shall be gay.
   I will charm every heart, in its crown I will sway,
   I woke from my dream and all idols was clay,
   And all portions of lovin' had all flown away

3. He taught me to love him and promised to love
   And cherish me over all other above,
   My poor heart is wondering, no misery can tell,
   He left me no warning, no words of farewell.

4. He taught me to love him and called me his flower,
   That was blooming to cheer him through life's weary hour,
   How I long to see him and regret the dark hour,
   He's gone and neglected his frail wildwood flower.

STRUM # 12

This is a 2/4 strum. Strum down on the 1st beat and down-up on the second. Repeat this pattern throughout the song.

Dixie

I___ wish I was- in the Land of cot-ton, old times there are soon for-got-ten Look a- way, look a - way, Look a-way, Dix ie- Land In Dix - ie Land - where I was born in, ear-ly on one Frost - y morn-ing Look a - way, look a way, look a - way, Dix-ie Land. Then I wish I was in Dix - ie Hoo - ray; Hoo- ray! In Dix - ie Land I'll take my stand to live or die in Dix - ie. A - way, a - way, a - way down south in Dix-ie, A - way, a - way, a - way down south in Dix - ie.

THE KEY OF A MINOR

THE BASIC CHORDS IN THE KEY OF A MINOR ARE: Am, Dm, and E7.

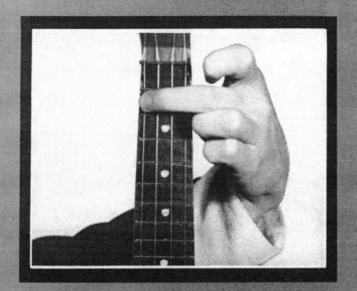
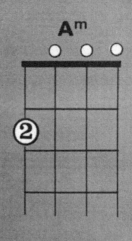

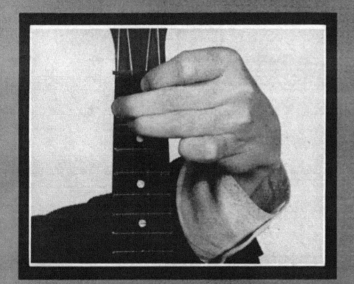
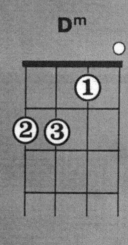

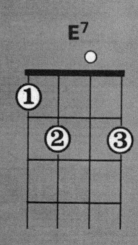

18

STRUM # 13

Count: 1-2 3 4-5 6
Strum: Down Up Down Up

In 6/8 time we have 6 beats per measure. Count 123, 456. With this strum, strum down on beats 1 and 2. Strum back on beat 3. Strum down again on beats 4 and 5. And back on beat 6.

Count: 1 2 3 4 5 6

6/8 Time =

Strum: 12 3 45 6
Down up Down up

When Johnny Comes Marching Home

2. The old church bell will peal with joy, Hurrah! (Am ... Em)
To welcome home our darling boy, Hurrah! Hurrah! (Am ... C)
The village lads and lassies gay (Am ... Dm)
With Roses they will strew the way, (Am ... E7)
And we'll all feel gay when Johnny comes marching home. (Am E7 Am E7 Am)

3. Get ready for the jubilee, Hurrah! Hurrah! (Am ... Em)
We'll give him a hero's three times three, Hurrah! Hurrah! (Am ... C)
The laurel wreath is ready now, (Am ... Dm)
To place upon his loyal brow, (Am ... E7)
And we'll all feel gay when Johnny comes marching home. (Am E7 Am E7 Am)

STRUM # 14

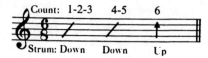

Strum down across the strings and let the chord ring for beats 1, 2, and 3. Strum down again and let the chord ring for beats 4 and 5. Strum back across the strings on beat 6.

High Barbaree

2. O are you a pirate or man o'war, cried we?
   Blow high! Blow low! And so sailed we.
   O no! I'm not a pirate, but a man o'war, cried he,
   A-sailing down all on the coasts of High Barbaree.

3. Then back up your topsails and heave your vessel to;
   Blow high! Blow low! And so sailed we.
   For we have got some letters to be carried home by you.
   A-sailing down all on the coasts of High Barbaree.

4. We'll be back up our topsails and heave our vessel to;
   Blow high! Blow low! And so sailed we.
   But only in some harbour and along the side of you.
   A-sailing down all on the coasts of High Barbaree.

5. For broadside, for broadside, they fought all on the main;
   Blow high! Blow low! And so sailed we.
   Until at last the frigate shot the pirate's mast away.
   A-sailing down all on the coasts of High Barbaree.

6. For quarters! for quarters! the saucy pirate cried.
   Blow high! Blow low! And so sailed we.
   The quarters that we showed them was to sink them in
   the Tide -A-sailing down all on the coasts of High Barbaree.

7. With cutlass and gun O we fought for hours three;
   Blow high! Blow low! And so sailed we.
   The ship it was their coffin, and their grave it was the sea.
   A-sailing down all on the coasts of High Barbaree.

8. But O! it was a cruel sight, and grieved us full sore,
   Blow high! Blow low! And so sailed we.
   To see them all a-drowning as they tried to swim to shore.
   A-sailing down all on the coasts of High Barbaree.

STRUM # 15

Strum down on 1. Strum down on the "and" of beat 1. Strum down on beat 2. And strum back up on the "and" of beat 2.

House Carpenter

1. Well met, Well met, you old true love, Well met, well met, said she. I have just re - turned from the sea shore sea From the land where the grass grows green. 2. Well — green.

Verses

2. Well, I could have married a king's daughter there,
And she would have married me,
But I refused the golden crown
And all for the sake of thee.
Chorus

3. 'If you could have married a king's daughter, there,
I'm sure you are to blame;
For I am married to a house carpenter
And I think he's a nice young man.'
Chorus

4. 'If you'll forsake your house carpenter
And come and go with me,
I'll take you where the grass grows green,
To the lands on the banks of the sea.
Chorus

5. She went an' picked up her sweet little babe,
And kissed it, one, two, three,
Sayin' stay at home with your father dear
And keep him good company.
Chorus

6. She went and dressed in her very best,
As, everyone could see;
She glittered and glistened and proudly she walked
The streets on the banks of the sea.
Chorus

7. They hadn't been sailing but about three weeks,
I'm sure it was not four,
Till this young lady began to weep,
And her weeping never ceased any more.
Chorus

8. 'Are you mourning for your house carpenter?
Are you mournin' for your store?'
'No I am mournin' for my sweet little babe
That I never will see any more.'
Chorus

9. They hadn't been sailing but about four weeks,
An' sure it was not more,
Till the ship sprang a leak from the bottom of the sea
And it sank to rise no more.
Chorus

THE KEY OF D

THE THREE BASIC CHORDS IN THE KEY OF D ARE: D, G, and A7.

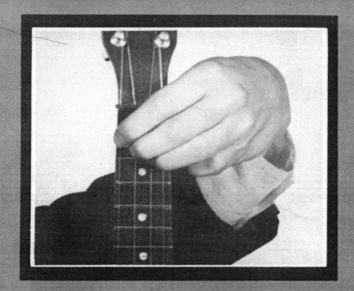

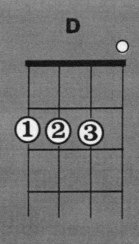

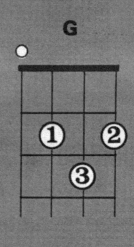

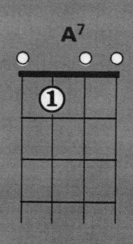

STRUM # 16

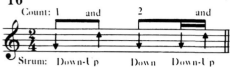

Strum down on 1 and up on the "and" of 1. Strum down on beat 2. and a fast down-up on the "and" of beat 2. This strum follows the rhythm of the 1st measure of the melody of Old Joe Clark.

Old Joe Clark

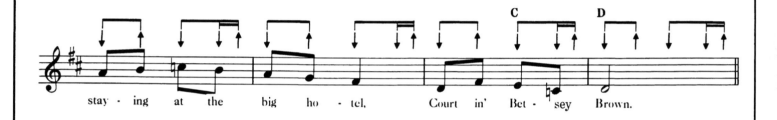

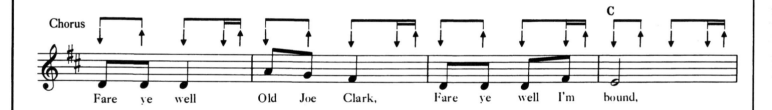

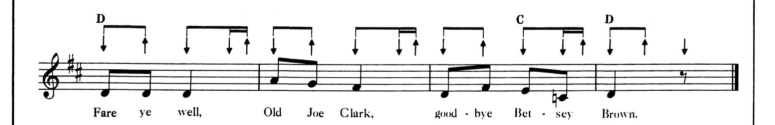

2. Old Joe Clark, the preacher's son,
   Preached all over the plain,
   The only text he ever knew
   Was "high, low jack and the game."

3. Old Joe Clark had a mule,
   His name was Morgan Brown,
   'And every tooth in that mule's head
   Was sixteen inches around.

4. Old Joe Clark had a house
   Fifteen stories high
   And every story in that house
   Was filled with chicken pie.

5. I went down to old Joe's house
   He invited me to supper,
   I stumped my toe on the table leg
   And stuck my nose in the butter.

THE F#m CHORD

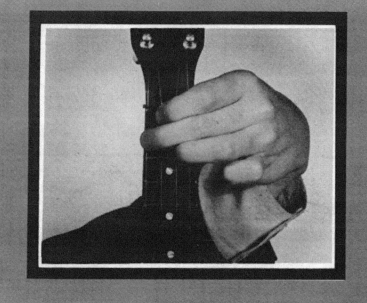
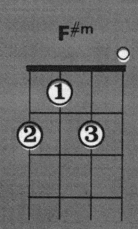

STRUM # 17

Count: 1and   2 and   3and   4 and

Strum: Down Down-Up Down Down-Up

Similar to strum #12 in 2/4, this strum is in 4/4 time. As used in this song, it should have a "swing" feeling.

Michael, Row the Boat Ashore

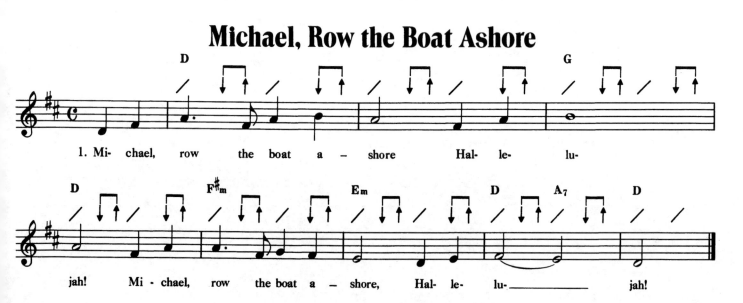

1. Mi- chael, row the boat a - shore Hal- le- lu-

jah! Mi - chael, row the boat a — shore, Hal- le- lu_____ jah!

2. Sister, Help to trim the sail, Hallelujah!
   Sister, Help to trim the sail, Hallelujah!
3. Jordan River is chilly and cold Hallelujah!
   Chills the body but not the soul, Hallelujah!
4. Jordan River is deep and wide Hallelujah!
   Milk and honey on the other side, Hallelujah!
5. I have heard the Good News too, Hallelujah!
   I have been born a new, Hallelujah!

STRUM # 18

STRUM #18 IN NOTATION

This strum is a syncopated, calypso-type pattern. Strum down on count "1-and." Let the chord ring for count 2. Strum up on the "and" of beat 2. And strum down on beats 3 and 4.

Kum Ba Ya
(Come by Here)

2. Someone's crying Lord, Kum-ba-ya.   (3 times)
   Oh, Lord, Kum-ba-ya.

3. Someone's praying Lord, Kum-ba-ya.   (3 times)
   Oh, Lord, Kum-ba-ya.

4. Someone's singing Lord, Kum-ba-ya.   (3 times)
   Oh, Lord, Kum-ba-ya.

STRUM # 19: "Classic" BALLAD STRUM

Strum down on beat 1. Let the chord ring for count 2. Strum down quickly on the "and" of beat 2. Strum down on beats 3 and 4.

STRUM # 19 IN NOTATION

Shenandoah

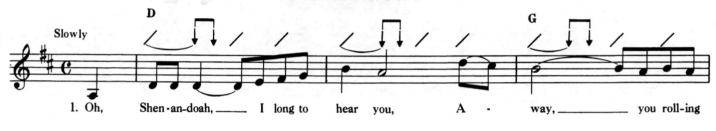

1. Oh, Shen-an-doah, ___ I long to hear you, A - way, ___ you roll-ing

riv - er, ___ Oh Shen-an-doah, ___ I long to hear you, A -

way, ___ we're bound a-way, Cross the wide Mis - sou - ri.

2. The white man loved the Indian maiden, (D)
Away, You rolling river (G D)
With notions His canoe was laden, (Bm D)
Away, We're bound away, (F#m)
"Cross the wide Missouri. (Bm D)

3. O, Shenandoah, I love your daughter, (D)
Away, You rolling river (G D)
I'll take her 'cross the rolling water, (Bm D)
Away, We're bound away, (F#m)
'Cross the wide Missouri (Bm D)

4. O, Shenandoah, I'm bound leave you, (D)
Away, You rolling river, (G D)
O, Shenandoah, I'll not Deceive you, (Bm D)
Away, We're bound away, (F#m)
'Cross the wide Missouri. (Bm D)

THE KEY OF E

THE THREE BASIC CHORDS IN THE KEY OF E ARE: E, A, and B7.

E

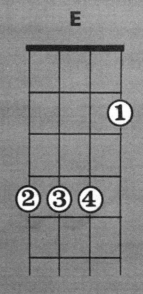

A

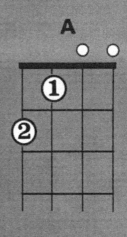

B⁷

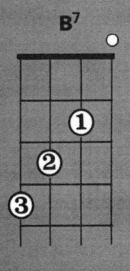

STRUM # 20: BLUES SHUFFLE

The Blues shuffle is a medium-slow pattern with a solid swing feeling. The musician strums down-up on each beat. This strum can best be illustrated by presenting it in 6/8 time.

ABOVE PLAYED AS:

Mamma Told Me Blues

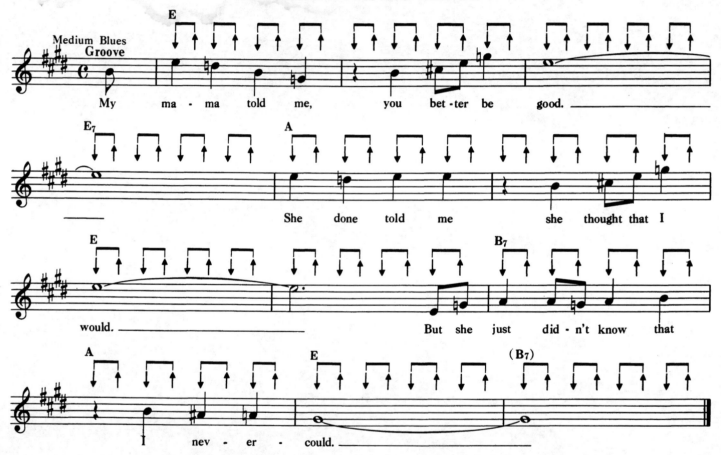

E   E₇
2. When I was sixteen - I traveled away.
A   E
I hit the city - I thought that I'd stay
   B₇
But I robbed Jackson's Food Store.
A   E
I couldn't pay.

E   E₇
3. The police grabbed me - before I could run.
A   E
They started shootin' - when they saw my gun.
   B₇   A   E
Oh I just didn't know that - crime was no fun.

E   E₇
4. I'm stuck in prison - some day I'll be free.
A   E
I won't go back - to that city.
   B₇
'Cause I know I'll remember
A   E
What mama told me.

STRUM # 21: FAST TEMPO SYNCOPATION

This is a syncopated strum pattern. Strum down on count "1 and." Strum down on 2 and back on the "and" of beat 2. Let the chord ring (don't strum) for count 3. Strum back up on the "and" of beat 3. Finally, strum down for beat 4.

Goin' Down the Road Feelin' Bad

2. I'm goin' where the climate suits my clothes   (3 times)
   And I'm sure gonna be feelin' better soon.

3. I'm goin' where the chilly winds don't blow,   (3 times)
   And I'm sure gonna be feelin' better soon.

4. I'm goin', where the Prince of Peace is King,   (3 times)
   And I'm sure gonna be feelin better soon.

5. I'm goin' to that Promised Land above,   (3 times)
   And I'm sure gonna be feelin' better soon.

THE KEY OF A

THE THREE BASIC CHORDS IN THE KEY OF A ARE: A, D, and E7.

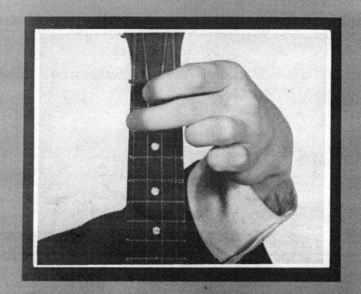

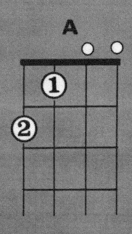

A

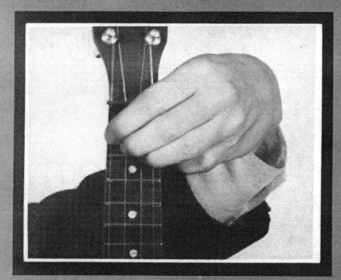

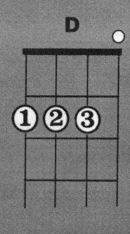

D

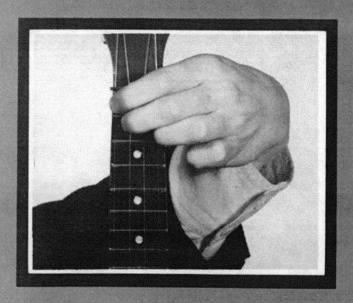

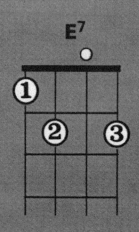

E[7]

STRUM # 22: TWO MEASURE SYNCOPATION

STRUM # 22 IN NOTATION

In strum #22, strum down on beats 1 and 2. Hold the chord for beat 3 (Don't strum.) Strum down on beat 4. In the second measure, strum down on beat 1. Strum down on beat 2 and strum up on the "and" of beat 2. Hold the chord for beat 3 (Don't Strum.) Strum back up on the "and" of beat three. Strum down on beat 4.

Worried Man Blues

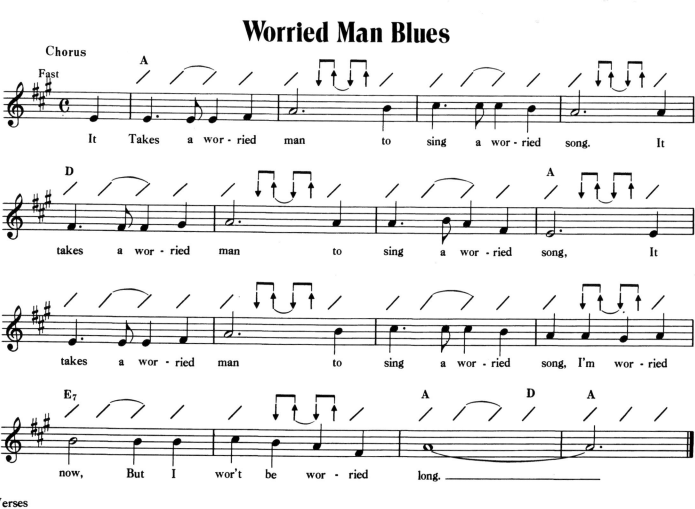

Verses

1. I went across the river, I lay down to sleep, (3 times)
When I woke up, had shackles on my feet.
Chorus

2. Twenty-nine links of chain around my leg, (3 times)
And on each link, an initial of my name.
Chorus

3. I asked that judge, tell me, what's gonna be my fine? (3 times)
Twenty-one years on the Rocky Mountain Line.
Chorus

4. Twenty-one years to pay my awful crime, (3 times)
Twenty-one years-but I got ninety-nine.
Chorus

5. The train arrived sixteen coaches long, (3 times)
The girl I love is on that train and gone.
Chorus

6. I looked down the track as far as I could see, (3 times)
Little bitty hand was waving after me.
Chorus

7. If anyone should ask you, who composed this song, (3 times)
Tell him was I, and I sing it all day long.
Chorus

STRUM # 23

Strum #23 is a ¾ time strum. Strum down-up on count 1. Strum down on counts 3 and 4.

Green Grow the Lilacs

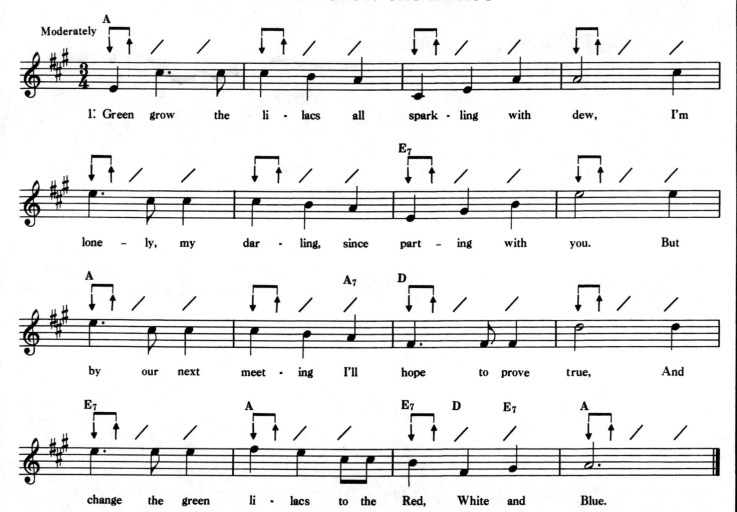

2. I used to have a sweetheart, But now I have none,
Since she's gone and left me, I care not for one.
Since she's gone and left me, Contented I'll be,
For she loves another one better than me.

3. I passed my love's window, Both early and late,
The look that she gave me, It made my heart ache
Oh, The look that she gave me was painful to see
For she loves another one better than me.

THE KEY OF F

THE THREE BASIC CHORDS IN THE KEY OF F ARE: F, Bb, and C7.

F

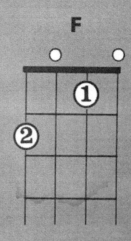

Bb

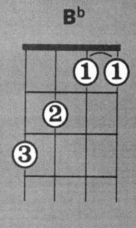

C7

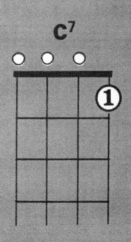

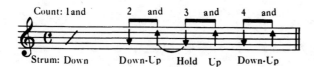

Strum down on beat 1. Strum down beat 2 and up on the "and" of 2. Let the chord ring for count 3 (Don't strum.) Strum up on the "and" of count 3. Strum down-up on beat 4.

Banks of the Ohio

Chorus
1. And on-ly say _____ that you'll be mine _____
_____ And in no oth _____ er arms en-twine, _____
_____ Down be-side _____ where the wa-ters flow _____
_____ A-long the banks _____ of the O-hi-o. _____

Verse 2. I asked my love to take a walk,
Just to walk a little way,
And as we walked and as we talked
About our coming wedding day.

Verse 3. I asked your mother for you, Dear,
And she said you were too young:
Only say that you'll be mine,
Happiness in my home you'll find.

STRUM #25

Count: 1and 2and 3and 4and   1 and 2 and 3 and 4and

Strum: Down Down Hold Down   Down-Up Down-Up Hold Up Down

STRUM #25 IN NOTATION

The only difference between this strum and pattern #22 is in the 2nd measure. In the second measure, strum down on count 1. Strum up on the "and" of count 1. Strum down on count 2. Strum up on the "and" of count 2. Let the chord ring on count 3 (Don't strum.) Strum back up on the "and" of count 3. And strum down on count 4.

No Hiding Place

2. The rock cried, "I'm Burning too." (F   B♭ C₇ F)
The rock cried, "I'm Burning too." (Dm G₇ C₇)
Oh, The rock cried out, "I'm buring too, (F)
I want to go to heaven the same as you," (B♭)
There's no hiding place down here. (F G₇ C₇ F)

3. The man cried, "I'm going too." (F   B♭ C₇ F)
The man cried, "I'm going too." (Dm G₇ C₇)
Oh, The man cried out, I'm going too, (F)
I want to go to heaven the same as you," (B♭)
There's no hiding place down here. (F G₇ C₇ F)

THE KEY OF Dm

THE THREE BASIC CHORDS IN THE KEY OF D MINOR ARE: Dm, Gm, and A7.

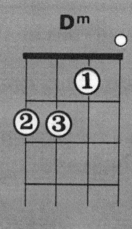

Dᵐ

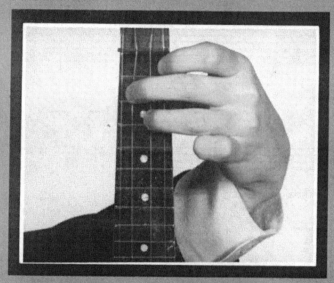
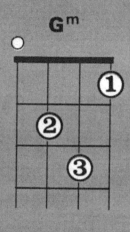

Gᵐ

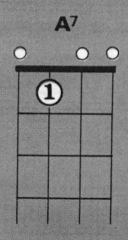

A⁷

STRUM # 26

Strum #26 is a 3/4 time strum. Strum down on beat 1.
Strum down-up on beats 2 and 3.

37

Henry Martin

2. And so He set sail till a ship He espied,
He gave Her the death shot for her.
Was chosen by lot to be one to go, To go, To be.
Robber of ships on the waves of the sea.
3. Three brothers in Scotland, With fortunes to seek,
Became only two in a week.
For Henry was captured for daring To be, To be,
Robber of ships on the waves of the sea.

STRUM # 27

Strum down on Beat 1. Strum down on beat 2. Hold beat 3. Strum down-up on beat 4. In the second measure. strum down on beat 1. Down-up on beat 2. And strum down on beats 3 and 4.

East Virginia

1. I was born _____ in East Vir____ gin____ ia

North Car - o - lin _____ a I did roam, _____

____ There I met _____ a - fair pret-ty maid - en,

Her name and age _____ I do not - know. _____

           Dm   G   Dm
2. Her hair it was of a brightsome color,
     Gm   Dm
And her lips of a ruby red,
     D   G Gm
On her breast she wore white lilies,
     Dm A7   Dm
There I longed to lay my head.

           Dm   G   Dm
3. Well. In my heart you are my darlin,'
     Gm   Dm
At my door you're welcome in,
     D   G Gm
At my gate I'll meet you my darlin,'
     Dm A7   Dm
If your love I could only win.

           Dm   G   Dm
4. Well in the night I'm dreamin' about you,
     Gm   Dm
In the day I find no rest,
     D   G Gm
Just the thought of you my darlin,'
     Dm A7   Dm
Sends aching pains all through my breast.

STRUM #28 ADDITIONAL SONGS

Strum #28 is the reverse of strum #22. The 2nd measure of strum #22 is the 1st measure of #28. The 1st measure of strum #22 is the second measure of #28.

Cruel War

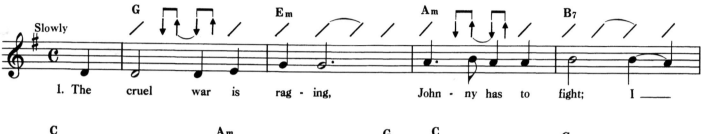

1. The cruel war is rag - ing, John - ny has to fight; I ____

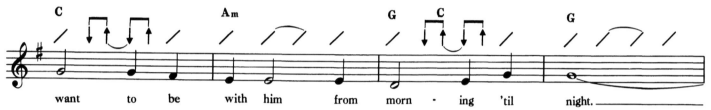

want to be with him from morn - ing 'til night. ____

____ I want to be with Him, It grieves ___ my heart so; "Won't you

let me go with you?" "No, my love no." ____

        G   Em   Am   B7
2. Tomorrow is Sunday, Monday is the day;
           C   Am   G C   G
   That your captain will call you, And you must obey.
         Em   Am   B7
   Your captain will call you, It grieves my heart so:
           C   Am   G C   G
  "Won't you let me go with you? No, My love no."
        G   Em   Am   B7
3. I'll tie back my hair, Men's clothing I'll put on;
          C   Am   G C   G
   I'll pass as your comrade, As we march along.
         Em   Am   B7
   I'll pass as your comrade, No one will ever know;
           C   Am   G C   G
  "Won't you let me go with you? No, My love no."

STRUM #29

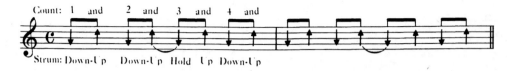

With strum #29, strum down-up on each beat. The "and" of beat 2 is tied to beat 3. Strum up on the "and" of count 3.

All My Trials

Verses

2. If living were a thing that money could buy.
The rich would live and the poor would die.

3. I've got a little book with pages three,
And every page spells liberty.

4. There grows a tree in paradise,
The pilgrim's call it the tree of life.